The TAO OF 52

Discovery of the Lost Science

—————————————Diallo Frazier

"Diallo Frazier has found a system that combines urban street smarts with practical applications to protect yourself. His method instills the confidence to handle a situation with relative ease once the principles are applied. Strikes to the most uncommon targets that instantly immobilize your assailant and makes him wish he'd thought twice before attacking you. The rhythmic moves appeal to the cultural movements of ancient Afrikan dances, sort of like a street version of Capoeira, except more direct and to the point."

(War Vet) Ret. Senior Master Sergeant (USAF) David Frazier. Aiki-Jujitsu Blackbelt, Certified JKD Instructor under Paul Vunak (PFS), Military Combat Certified; also holds the title of "BMF."

"Do not pray for an easy life, pray for the strength to endure a difficult one."

Bruce Lee

52 Blocks was developed during slavery at the time of the slave fights of the 1800s. In the beginning, it was called, "Virginia Scufflin'." Virginia Scufflers were the enslaved Warriors that would fight for the Freedom of their families, self-liberation, and to reunite with their families. These principles became the foundation of 52 Blocks. A 52 Block warrior is taught in the beginning that you are to fight for freedom, family, liberations, and unity. The very principles that the slave fighters fought for in the days of Virginia Scuffling became the spiritual principles of the evolved 52 Blocks. The enslaved fighters were men who were trained in the different ways of Nubian Combat systems. These systems eventually molded into one style which at the time was known as Virginia Scufflin'. These men became legendary; they would be equivalent to today's top MMA warriors, except the reward was not money, but better slave quarters, rights to bring their families back together, or possibly buying their families freedom. So, Virginia Scrufflers began to take moves from the best of the fighters they fought or saw fight because any advantage they could have in winning a fight might mean freedom for his family. Some of the styles said to have been used during those times were Borey, Reisy, and Hausa Boxing. These combat systems were rites of passage for the different Nubian Warriors from the Fatherland, so it was commonplace for the young Nubians to be skilled in combat. Now, let's examine the fighting systems that formed what we know as Virginia Scufflin', and how 52 techniques derive from these arts. First Borey, a standup grappling art of the Mandinka warriors. The art incorporates knees, headbutts, grabs, kicks, and bone-breaking holds. These are all tools used and taught in today's modern 52 Blocks system within the Gangsta Locks and Moving Bodies techniques of 52 Hand Blocks. Virginia Scufflin' is rooted in the original arts of the Captured Warriors of the Middle Passage. When practicing this art, we not only uplift ourselves, but we uplift the ancestors who fought for our spirits to be free of stress, oppression, and chaos. 52 Blocks is rooted in what was known as Virginia Scufflin' and Virginia Scufflin' is rooted in the arts of the Fatherland. This

is why we discuss the Grandfather arts from the Warriors of the Middle Passage.

The next art we will discuss is Hausa Boxing as it is named today. Hausa Boxing is considered to be the Cousin of Kemetic Boxing. Hausa Boxing is a Knuckle game system originated in Nigeria that utilizes punches such as the jab, cross, and uppercut but it also implements knees, head butts, and kicks. Tools that are used in 52 with the Ghetto Boxing as well as our Head Fight game. We learn that these were also the weapons of the Virginia Scuffler, the combat system that 52 is derived from.

The last Fatherland combat system that we are discussing will be Reisy. Reisy is the deadly Head-Butting style that was developed by the warriors of Eritrea. Reisy uses stand up grappling movements to control the enemy so that you can destroy them with the Big Knuckle or head. The Big Knuckle is used with deliberate actions. Meaning, we have targeted striking areas of attack during close quarter combat that 52 specializes in. 52 Blocks has taken from the system of Reisy but does not use the whole system, but we see the foundation of our head fighting technique derive from the Eritrea warrior combat style. The ancestors of 52 Hand Blocks speak to us through the language of combat. The tools we learn tell us the history of a warrior culture. From our head fighting to Slap boxing, it is all rooted in an Original Nubian combat system that cocooned into a hybrid system called, Virginia Scufflin' then transformed into Jail House Rock, only to be resurrected as 52 Hand Blocks.

—"Let the Lord Judge the Criminals."

Tupac Shakur

Mastered in Prison

June 18, 1865, in the state of Texas, on the balcony of Galveston's, Ashton Villa General, Gorgan Granger read the contents of General Order NO. 3 which said that slaves are now working men and women, to no longer be oppressed under the guides of slavery (I am paraphrasing). Thus, was the end of legal slavery and the birth of the Prison Industrial Complex. With this end to slavery came Black Codes in the southern states. These black codes would be the reason for the transformation of Virginia Scufflin' becoming a jailhouse system. Virginia Scufflers made their way into the prison systems of the south, thanks to Black Code. Black Codes were laws based on slavery codes put together to continue the slave labor and keep free Nubians from building their own communities of powerful and educated Warriors and Queens. With the Black Code in play, the prison system became the new money maker, using prison slave labor to make back the slave money lost in the Civil War. So, we see many black men enter the prison system at a high rate starting in late 1865, and Virginia Scufflers were among these men. It is said that the Virginia Scufflers were very defiant prisoners and some punishments for these men were being put in cells with inmates that were promised to be rewarded if they "taught" these defiant negroes a lesson. But the opposite is what would happen. The Virginia Scufflers were the ones who conducted a class in these cells. Soon word of their defiant mentality and physical dominance began to circulate through the prisons amongst the inmates. Some searched them out and very few were taught the art of Virginia Scufflin', but the ones who were taught were taught in secret.

The system began to also adjust to the environment it was in. It began to transform into a close quarter combat system that was also about being able to use the environment as a weapon. From walls, bed posts', shanks, shoestrings, and eating utensils, the new Virginia Scuffler could transform anything into a weapon of offensive defense. Move into the 30s and 40s where Virginia Scufflin' changes into Jail House Rock or JHR. Jail House Rock becomes the new system of combat, it is the new hybrid system that is only practiced and taught behind the wall, later to make its way into the black Ghettos of America. When brothas would get out of prison, after being incarcerated due to the Jim Crow laws that replaced Black Code, many of them decided to move out of the Southern States of America. Many migrated to the East, West, and Midwest states. The cities famous for JHR practitioners were Chicago, Brooklyn, Bronx, St. Louis, Detroit, Oakland, Atlanta, and Los Angeles. JHR practitioners that migrated from the south would also teach their sons and other young men JHR basics. These basics became culture rites of passage for many young men, from slap boxing to playing body. It was all JHR basic training methods that became fun games and learning tools for young black men in the Hood. Starting in the 50s and 1960s, when the black revolution began to take hold, the Jim Crow laws in the south were still in effect, but in the East, West and Mid-West, there was the problem of Police brutality and racial profiling. This put black males in jail at an alarming rate, which also became the rebirth of Jail House Rock into the prison systems. It had never left the jail system, it was just brought back to the forefront. With the Civil Rights Movement of the 60s and the Anti-War Movements of this time, we begin to see jailing of Blacks, Chicanos, Native Americans, and other minorities on the rise.

By 1966, the Black Power Movement went to another level with the forming of the Black Panther Party; with their intelligent defiance and physical presence, the police setups and convictions went to a new high. Not just against Panthers, but any other grassroots movement groups in oppressed communities. On March, 1968, the government's Counterintelligence Program or COINTEL PRO put out a document that listed one of their top priorities was to PREVENT THE RISE OF A BLACK MESSIAH who could unify and electrify the militant Black Nationalist Movement. When this memo was released, the F.B.I and local police began to go hard on the black community with the legal system. Nubians again began to be arrested at high rates. They were also given longer jail sentences than any of their counterparts. Due to the large volume of black men being put in jail, the overcrowding began to also create an even more volatile prison environment than before. This was the environment of JHR coming back to the forefront. Now, you not only had criminals in jail, but you begin to have a high volume of revolutionaries in jail. In the same cells as the hustlas, pimps, and drug dealers that they ran out of the hood. Jail House Rock became a serious tool of defense for all.

Jail House Rock changed from JHR to 52 Hand Blocks in the mid-1960s in New York. It was renamed 52 after the card game, 52 Hand Blocks in the mid-1960s in New York. It was renamed 52 after the card game, 52 Pick Up, a childhood game played to pass the time by inmates. In the game, you throw the deck of cards on the floor and the second person has to pick them back in-suite order. So, 52 stands for 'let the cards lay were they may or anything goes' because when the deck falls, there is no rule of order as it hits the floor. The Blocks part of 52 represents the attacks and counters that we used as the offensive defense in our system. The Blocks are the Windshield Wiper, Shufflin' the Deck, Skull, and Crossbones, Windmill, Crossing the L, Peek-A-Boo, Wall Spring, Wall Walk, Speed Bag, Single and Double Leg Pant Flip, Shoulder Brush, Up Rock, etc. These techniques are our blocks, but a Block for a 52 practitioner is actually an attack more than it is a simple block used just to stop an assault against us. The reason 52 was mastered in prison is because of the real-life application it had to go through. The practitioners of this art used it in the deadliest of environments. Having to fight for life preservation, not fame, sport, or material gain puts a sense of urgency to your training, knowing the anxiety of death will change the method and training of a 52 Blocks Instructor or student. In prison, 52 has become a combat system of adaptability, and a vicious mentality. Knowing if you lose it may mean death or severe injury, changes the mindset of a man. Therefore, the humiliation and deadly force become a factor in the 52 game. You as a 52 practitioner want to humiliate and inflict severe damage to the enemy in a quick amount of time. The humiliation is done to give a warning to all others who dare to challenge you and the quick time is so that a C.O or the enemy's allies are not able to prevent the destruction of the adversary. The Jail House 52 Blocks is used in closed quarters so the infighting of 52 gets better and more evolved as it trains to fight in cells, closets, and hallways. Focusing on elbows, stomps, and head fighting became necessary to be able to fight in handcuffs and shackles.

These techniques originated from the days of slave combat. Our enslaved Nubian ancestors would have to figure out ways to do battle while in shackles that were attached to their wrists, ankles, and necks. Their warrior spirits would find a way to fight against slave traders on ships as well as at slave ports in the Caribbean, so learning how to revolt with shackles attached to your main tools of defense became a part of combat.

Those blueprint combat techniques remained a staple in the new system of JHR and 52 Blocks. Our in-fight game with heel stomps, peek-a-boo blocks and guard breaks, pinching bites, and targeting strikes all grow out of necessity to know how to defend and attack while being shackled in handcuffs. Another aspect of 52 training is our workouts. The iron body callisthenic workouts of 52Blocks from pushups, body squats, burpees, sit-ups, playing body, and the most noted of all, the bar ~~techniques~~techniques, or pull-ups. These exercises became a staple in the training of the warriors behind the wall while eating tuna, oysters and noodles in "spreads" would help build muscle from the protein intake and providing energy from the carbohydrates. The 52 Block prison Warrior perfected his body so he could perfect his art. He knew that if his body was perfected through combat workouts and his mind was trained to never quit because of pain and struggle, then how could anyone defeat an Iron Body and Steel Mind. The pain, violence, and suffering of prison life molded the training and delivery of 52 Hand Blocks techniques into a refined rage of offensive defense. So, 52 Blocks was perfected in an environment where war is the norm and peace is rare, so to fight in chaos to a 52 Blocks warrior is to fight at home. 52 was born out of Pain, Oppression and Struggle; these obstacles became the fuel for the 52 Blocks practitioner to become great at everything we do while doing it with style.

"Happy to be Free because the streets are the place for a playa to be."

Ice T

Perfected On The Streets

Beginning in the mid-1970s, we see 52 Blocks really hitting the streets around the different hoods across America. We really don't know why at this time, it explodes on the streets, but the practice of 52 in some way is seen from Philadelphia to Oakland. With the spread of 52 across the country, we also see the style being expressed differently from region to region. From the New York hand and arm attacks, the deadly elbow attacks of Atlanta's Alto 52, or the Head fighting of "Chi-Town" and the heal stomps and kicks found in L.A., each region may have the same general tools, but because of environment, different tools became more of a focus of the art from city to city. 52 on the street is no longer just about using it in a closed quarter situation. It changes footwork to a level of angling and more suited for a more open space fighting. 52 begins to do what it has always done, keep its essence but adjust to its environment. On the street, we begin to hear people refer to 52 as a "pretty boy art" due to its ~~rhythmatic~~rhythmic movements, beautiful attacks, and flashy counters. 52 was reborn when on the streets, it had taken a turn to a more free-flowing style that emphasized 'Rhythm of Self'. Rhythm of Self is a key component in 52; it is the fighting beat that you discover by training with music to find your own fighting rhythm. Rhythm of Self enables us as warriors to be even more self-expressive while engaging in harmonious combat. Making the fight become more of an unpredictable dance than a choreographed march that is easily timed and countered. Rhythm of Self creates an element of surprise for the enemy you are facing. You will be hard to figure out in the midst of combat because when you have trained in changing rhythms, you are able to change the tempo of a fight at any given moment. You begin to use pausing amid the fight to slow the fight down or engage in an up-tempo exchange to make the enemy fight in chaos if he is used to fighting in an organized way. Rhythm of Self always allows us to control the fight through timing and tempo. On the street, the

52 Block practitioner is also no longer in a controlled, violent environment, he is now in an environment that can have peaceful times for long periods. This peace has to be a challenge for the 52 Blocks warrior. He must know that even though danger is no longer at every corner, he must still prepare himself for it. So, to keep his discipline on the street with the same intensity as he did being locked up becomes a challenge of self-perfection as a warrior, we must remind ourselves that our families still need protection, as well as our spouses. We have to find reasons to keep up our discipline of training and eating right. The psychological fight that freedom takes you through becomes a challenge in itself. For those who have learned 52 on the streets and never have been behind the Wall, your training has always been intense and focused on the dangers of everyday street life. Freedoms that you are used to, and pressures of your peers have large challenges also, Challenges from not engaging in bad behavior, to being too comfortable around those who are not comrades. Knowing to be on guard at all times, never letting your environment get the best of you are all lessons to be learned and maintained while on the streets. The fight training is also the difference of 52 being perfected on the streets. On the streets, you are able to train and practice your art with different styles of fighting. Training with the different practitioners of combat helps you to see where there may be holes in your 52 game. So, by sparring with different styles, we begin to be able to adjust 52 to all styles of combat. By having a weakness exposed in a safe controlled environment, we can make what was once a flaw in our game, into an attribute. Not having to hide your training and being able to share combat techniques with others, builds your 52 Blocks skills to a level of perfection. While on the streets, 52 practitioners are also now able to contemplate the depth of the mental training of 52 and it's philosophies. 52 is a physical combat system that developed into a mental philosophy. The philosophical lessons of 52 are taken from the physical hardships of struggle that 52 Blocks was created from. The street 52Blocks practitioner begins to study the mindset of the Original Virginia Scufflers, this creates a deeper level of philosophy and combat awareness in the 52 community. This perfection is enabled by street living and not cell block survival, so

street knowledge mixed with spirituality developed a new warrior mentality. One of the main influences on the mindset of the street 52 Blocks warrior was the 5% brothas, they practiced 52 Blocks but redefined it as GOD Blocks. Five Percenters are called 5% because 85% of society is being led astray and oppressed by 10 % of society. Then there is the 5% that educate and uplift the masses, these are the Poor Righteous Teachers or the 5% Nation. 52 was called God Blocks because in the science of Supreme math; the number 7 is the number of GOD. When you add 5 and 2 you get 7, so 52 Blocks was also known as GOD Blocks. Sense 52 was created in the womb of oppression, struggle, love, and pain, it seemed fitting for it to be called GOD Blocks because only GOD could have protected the people through our struggle. The Blocks were developed to protect the God body while going through hell, this is the reason we develop Steel Minds to study the strengths and weaknesses of any enemy. We develop Iron Bodies to be able to carry out the minds will, as well as developing spiritual insight so our spirit can will our bodies and minds to keep going when it seems we should be finished. This mindset was a change in 52 because it created discipline on the streets amongst 52 practitioners around the country. The influence of the Nation of Gods and Earths can still be felt to this day in the discipline of modern52 Blocks. Thus, we see how the street perfected 52 Blocks, know that the freedom of the street will continue to redefine and build 52 to even higher levels of combat discipline. The 21st century 52 will be a system that is hybrid, as we have seen with Zab Juda using 52 to freeze Mayweather in the third round of their fight or how Rashad Evans uses the footwork and rhythm of 52 to enhance his MMA skills. The next step in the future, you will see 52 blend physical and philosophical techniques of other arts but keep the rhythm of 52 Blocks.

—————————————————"You have to be like a Quarterback playing the
Safety position."

                                            —————————————————Kiongozi Diallo
Frazier

Offensive Defense

All combat practitioners use defense, but most don't use their defense as their offensive. The 52 Blocks Warrior knows that his defense is an attacking defense, therefore we say offensive defense. When the 52 Blocks man defends, his mind is on causing the enemy pain with a defensive attack. This enables us to find an offensive opening to create our counterattacks which is our offense. A 52 Blocks practitioner knows that pausing between attacks, countering, and peripheral attacks are all used in the development of an attacking defense. The attacking defense is aided when we train the main tools of defensive attacks which are the techniques that I just mentioned. Having the ability to counter an enemy will enable the 52 man to know his enemy's abilities without the enemy being able to figure you out. The enemy is not able to figure you out because when they are attacking, they are focused on your destruction not your capabilities as a fighter. But by us countering we are letting the enemy reveal himself to us, so we can figure out his rhythm and his main tools of combat. One of the most important parts of combat is counter striking, this is also one of the most neglected areas of training. For a 52 Blocks practitioner, countering is a way of life. Counter striking enables us to strike the enemy at his strongest and weakest points. It's his strongest offensive state but it is his weakest defensive state. The reason behind this is because when a non-counter fighter attacks, he usually lets his defense relax. The moment the attacker relaxes his defense is the moment that the 52 counter strike comes into play to expose the weakness of his attack. This is our attacking defense. When countering the enemy, you cause confusion in his mind. This is valid because once the enemy has committed to his attack, he believes in that strike so much that he lets down his defense. So, when you counter and hit him at that moment, you knock the confidence out of his mind; he begins to feel open to your attacks which makes him question his own speed and overestimate your speed. He has been fooled by the art of counter striking, usually, this frustrates the enemy and makes him go into a duck and cover mode. Or they begin to just charge you out of frustration from your counter striking but ducking and charging only makes the fight easier for the 52 Blocks man to pick apart the enemy. The counter will make the enemy lose his emotional control. When he loses control, it becomes a simpler fight for us as 52 practitioners to destroy him with our controlled, calculating Offensive defense.

The next factor in our Offensive Defense that we will discuss is tempo control during the fight. The tempo is the speed, timing, and quickness that is used in the fog of war. When talking about these factors one must know that they are controlled by the pause factor and reaction timing. Let us cover reaction timing first, reaction timing is based on how quickly the mind registers an attack and how fast your instinctive response is. If one has trained their 52 Blocks techniques properly, their response will be quick and violent, if you haven't trained your mind and body properly, you will think before the attack and this can lead to defeat. How can one train proper instinctive reactions so that you are no longer thinking in a fight, but only acting through instinct? We can do this by retraining our autonomic responses to pain or attacks. Autonomics is the body's visceral nervous system that controls the involuntary actions of the body, such as breathing, eye blinking, crying, and most importantly, for the 52 Blocks Warrior, one's reaction to pain. We retrain our autonomic responses by having a training partner attack us, without us defending the attack at first. This is done to see what your natural response to a punch, kick knee, head butt, elbow, or bite is. Once we have identified our natural response then we begin to create our attacking response to these same blows. This is done by changing your instincts through repetition. Get punched in the face by your training partner and react violently to it. Whether it's by answering the punch with an elbow or returning the favor with a punch of your own. You must retrain all pain reactions from bending, kneeling, slumping, or grabbing your area of pain into punching, controlling, kicking, elbowing, and head fighting the enemy when any pain is felt. This creates reaction timing in your mindset, so the body and mind are always thinking offensive defense when it comes to an attack or your response to pain. Now, let us discuss the pause factor of fighting. The pause factor is the time that you allow to happen between strikes. The pause can be quick, or it can be drawn out depending on what the enemy's strengths may be. We as 52 Blocks warriors need to be able to recognize a weakness is the enemies main tool of combat, so when countering with pausing we use long pauses to slow down the fast man and we use quick pauses between punches to overwhelm the slower man. The slower pause will make a fight seem to be at a break to the enemy, but it is only slowed to make the enemy relax his guard if only for one second, so we may strike in a millisecond once we see our opening. The quick pause is used to overwhelm your enemy; quick pausing is a method of simply having a continuous forward attack against the enemy. The more attacks toward the enemy, the higher your chances for their destruction. Momentum and timing are elements in offensive-defensive that help us dominate the fight. Timing enables us to strike at opportune moments that will create a feeling of off-balance by the enemy, weakening his confidence. The timing of the attack will transform into momentum for the 52 Blocks warrior. When the timing attack is executed with all your strength and power, the momentum will be a downhill feeling for us and an uphill struggle for the enemy. Never allow bad timing to stop your combat momentum. This can be done by practicing organized timing attacks from different angles and scenarios, making counter timing an instinctive action. 52 is called the art of Defense because of the elements we have discussed earlier, but the defense of a 52 Blocks practitioner is meant not to simply stop or avoid an attack, instead, it is meant to destroy the oncoming attack. This attacking defense is what separates 52 from other combat systems and is the essence of our system's Offensive Defense. The last element in our offensive defense is peripheral attacks or no-look strikes. We use no-look attacks to draw the enemy into a comfort state that will enable us to catch them off guard. We use our peripheral vision to keep eye contact with the enemy but making him think we are retreating or unaware of their movements while we are actually countering their attack. With the peripheral counter, the enemy is attacked without them being able to prepare for the hit. This will weaken his confidence and make him overly cautious when he wants to attack, even if he sees an opening. Peripheral attacks create a mental defense for the 52 Blocks practitioner because the enemy will always think you are trying to draw them into an attack by leaving an opening. So, they will hesitate before they commit to an attack, creating a mental defense for the 52 blocks practitioner. Our Offensive Defense ranges from physical to mental warfare. Know the element of Offensive Defense and watch your skills grow to an enlightened level.

————————"Your work is to discover your work and then with all your heart give yourself to it."

Unknown

Iron Body

A 52 Blocks man should always train for chaos and ruff footing. If you train to fight stable in an unstable environment, then stability for you will be every environment. Train in hot humid environments, on soft sand, with obstacles in your way, or in cold weather. Make your training processes as uncomfortable and as hard as possible. This will make the fight that much easier and it will enable us to take the enemy into an uncomfortable realm for them and familiarity for us. Create chaos in your training, loud noise, talk aggressively to your training partner while training, fight more than one attacker at a time during your training, then fight from range to range. The 52 Blocks practitioner must have his inner rhythm set to a pace that is unusual to most fighters. This is how we gain an advantage in combat. This type of training creates muscle memory for your fast twitch and slow twitch muscles. Which are needed to change the pace and timing of a fight. We train our muscles to respond quickly and efficiently when we train in chaos. They began to respond more effectively in the chaotic scramble that we call combat. This type of training must also be accompanied by resistance training and functional resistance training. Resistance training is something that most combat practitioners implement in their training, but functional resistance training is not as common as it should be. Functional resistance training is a training method that will create muscle memory for actual power and delivery to the enemy. This is accomplished by not having a rest time between resistance sets, but rather work the method of attack that best fit the muscle group you have exercised. For example, if you work your pectoral major muscle with resistance training instead of resting after the set, you would work your Bumrush, creating a memory for your muscles to hit with the same strength that you used to do push-ups or bench press. This will create a functional power and do away with stationary strength. You will put weights on your hands and hit the mitts and shadow box. This will enhance your speed and power punches. Ankle weights are used for knee and kicking training, doing the same normal knees and kicks, just adding weight to your ankles will bring out the functional muscle memory to your knees and kicks. That will create a more brutal counter strike. Wearing a weight vest during slap boxing, light sparring sessions and footwork drills will create better balance, center of gravity, and quick feet reaction timing. These are all functional resistance training methods of the 52 Blocks warrior that keeps us balanced and the enemy off balanced. These methods of functional muscle training are targeting our high motion combat tools which are our head, legs, arms, hands, and feet. Now, let's talk about Iron Body training for the low motion parts of the body, which is our center; back, chest, and stomach. Training to strengthen your center or low motion parts of the body is probably the most important defensive training you can do. Now, why do 52 practitioners spend so much time training their backs, chest, and stomach? Well, because that's where there is limited motion. These areas become weak points in battle and strong targeting areas for the enemy to attack. These areas of low motion are also protecting vital organs that when damaged can cause death or severe injury. Knowing these things, the 52 Blocks man keeps his center strong and ready. Training to be able to handle punishment to the body, as well as how to avoid damage, so he trains the muscles of his center appropriately. These are just a few training methods for the center that we do. Nothing fancy or new, just extremely effective.

Ab Workout- 30 of each exercise

1. Hanging Torso Twist	7. Burpees
2. Sit Up ceiling touches	8. Leg Raises
3. V-Ups	9. Bent over 45 twist
4. Medicine Ball Twist	10. Hanging V-Ups
5. Weight Bar Twist	11. Hanging Knee raises
6. Medicine Ball drops	12. Medicine Ball stomach rolls

Chest and Back Workout -30 of each exercise

1. Incline pushups	5. Medicine Ball alternating push-ups
2. Decline Pushups	6. Pyramid pushups
3. Dips	7. Goin' Body for 3 two-minute rounds.
4. Pull-Ups	

—————————————"Stay wise and the mind is untouchable."

Rakim

Steel Mind

For the 52 Blocks warrior to achieve completeness as a human being, they must first learn to be at peace with their own reality. If you can't live on this earth's plain with complete peace, then you will never find your purpose. When I say peace, I don't mean having no other emotion but happiness, the peace that I am speaking of means to be able to overstand your circumstances in the now and from there be able to make a plan of action to achieve the best out of yourself. We are not all the same, some have the gift of athletic ability, some strength and others are cerebral. The thing is to find out your best attribute and capitalize on your strengths. When we come to this overstanding, then we will know peace not only during combat but in life. Once we have found our gift, we must live in that realm of reality instead of existing in a realm of confusion, because of our lack of comprehension of who we are as a human being. In the words of Bruce Lee, "We must find the cause of our ignorance." So, we can liberate ourselves from undisciplined fighting and living. When the 52 man has done this, he will draw himself closer to universal comprehension and combat stillness. Combat stillness is the peace that one feels physically and mentally during the fight. Your mind is focused on the enemy but not focused on technique. Your body is in action but not acting just being; this is the definition of combat stillness. Being a 52 practitioner, one must also have a complete awareness of death and what it is, so we have no worry of it during combat. If one has no overstanding of death, then you will never live and fight the way you should. When one has studied death, then life is always with him, and the warrior should know this in his heart. With the study and overstanding of death, the worry and anxiety of it begins to be eliminated. When the warrior sees death for what it is, just a next step to life, then we realize that death, in fact, is an illusion and there is only life. When this enlightenment is reached, the 52 warrior will always give himself to life and combat wholeheartedly. For one to have eternal life, one must die by the flesh and to die one must be born into life. The two are actually one and there is completeness in their opposites. Know what life is, so you will know what death is not.

————————————   "The building of the strong is the lessons
for the meek"

X-Clan

Rules of Hood Warfare

Rule 1. Always listen before you talk, look before you walk and observe before you stalk. The meaning of the first part of rule one, "Listen before you talk" is this; we must always listen to gather intel on the subject on which we speak, whether it be on the attack of the enemy or the knowledge of a work topic being expressed. We must not make a fool of ourselves or put our allies in a bad situation because we didn't listen to the details of a discussion. To "Look before you walk" means to have complete awareness of your surroundings. If you enter a room, recognize were the exits are, pay attention to the potential threats that are around, whether it be people or objects. If you are in your car, pay attention to the rearview mirrors so you can avoid predators. To look before you walk is to have complete comprehension of your environment. The last part of rule one is to "Observe before you stalk." To observe before you stalk means to take note of the preys habits, strengths, weaknesses, and allies, so you can use that information to your advantage. Whether we are talking about a professional fighter who has to observe before he stalks his next opponent. The professional fighter will study tape on the opponent and learn his strengths and weaknesses. This is a method of observing before you stalk. If we are talking about an office environment you as an office manager might want a Senior Management position, so you have to observe the person who is in your way. You study the positive and negative sides of their management skills. What amount of money they are making the company, how much money they are saving the company, what hours they keep and how they interact with the staff and their work ethic. These are all things you will learn about the opposition when observing their habits so you will surpass them during your stalking of their position. From a revolutionary perspective, if you want to move any drugs out of your community, you would have to observe the fiends because they will always lead you to the drug dealer. From there you would observe the habits and route of the drug dealer because he will lead you to his supplier. Then the habits of the drug dealer will teach you how to stalk a supplier to eliminate him from the equation. I have given you different scenarios to the meaning of Observe before you stalk, so you may have proper overstanding of the concept.

Rule. 2 In war you must follow the commands of your higher ranking Soulja. It is designed this way for order, the higher-ranking Officer is given more intelligence on the attack or defense than the lower ranking Soulja. We must learn to follow orders so we will know how to give them in the future.

Rule. 3 Never make emotional decisions, it will always lead to defeat. Emotions negate logical thought; if one operates on his emotions then he is most likely to make irrational moves. Emotions such as love, hate, revenge, and worry will prevent you from considering all possibilities and solutions to the problem at hand. For example, if you work for a corporation and you get written up for project that went bad because of the person you delegated a section of the work to fail their assignment, your emotional decision may be to punch the person in the mouth and if followed, it will lead you to jail and the unemployment line. This is what is meant when we say emotional decisions will lead to defeat. You may win a battle with emotions but never a war.

Rule.4 What is pain to a warrior but a privilege. Pain and the_-ability to handle pain is a measure of a warriors heart. Pain is Life! The more a man can endure in this struggle called life, the more he can also overcome. Pain breeds strength in the hearts, minds, and souls of warriors. When one is stricken with pain, they are reminded of the strength of the human will.

————Rule.5 There is no greater sin in warfare than ignorance. Ignorance by definition is destitute of knowledge or education. So, lacking knowledge of your enemy or adversary can lead to your defeat. Preparing yourself for battle by not educating yourself to the times and your environment is the preparation of a fool.

Rule.6 Beware of those who talk loud but do little in time of war. These people are the friends of the enemy. Those who consistently talk have two major attributes; either they are worried about the situation and are trying to use the "Blow Fish" technique to blend into the crowd in hopes not to have to actually fight. Or they are knuckleheads that don't know how to follow orders and rules of combat. Their lack of discipline can be more damaging in war than the cowardice of the "Blow Fish."

―――――――――――Rule.7   Silence and observation are major weapons of defense.

The more you know about them the better chances you have at being victorious against the enemy because you have knowledge of their strengths and weaknesses. The less the enemy knows about you the better chance of them bowing down to you, because of a lack of knowledge on your capabilities.

These are the rules of Hood Warfare, take them, and use the knowledge to discipline yourself and the warriors around you. Y.G's need the lessons of the O.G's so they can keep the legacy of Hood Discipline alive. If we don't know our true foundations, then the hood will be destroyed.

"Be peaceful, be courteous, obey the law, respect everyone; but if someone   puts their hands on you, send him to the cemetery."

Malcolm X

52 Blocks Code of Combat

These are the things our ancestors fought for and what we as 52 Blocks warriors continue to fight for.

1. Freedom- The right to live a righteous, natural, law-abiding life without being

harassed, oppressed, jailed, or killed for living freely.

2. Family- We fight for our families' freedom in the future; family are the ones that

have your back in bad times even more than they do in good times.

3. Liberation- To break away from oppressive thoughts, behaviors, and practices.

4. Unity- Peace, liberty, and alliance among all oppressed people no matter their

race, religion, sex, class, or nationality.

"The fight is won or lost far away from witnesses- behind the lines, in the gym and out there on the road, long before I dance under those lights."

————Muhammad
Ali

Internalized Combat

We don't want to learn 52 Blocks, if you learn 52 you may have some movements, techniques and strikes but they are not you. When you learn a system, you may hesitate to use the tools you have learned, because what you have learned is separate from you. It is an accessory to be shown off to impress others or for blowfish use. But when we internalize our art it will be a part of your spirit and soul. When you walk you will move as a 52 man, when you speak your words will flow with a 52 style, and when you fight your rhythm and timing will express the artistic beauty of 52 Blocks. Once internalized, there will never be any hesitation or thought about the 52 Block technique. There will only be the human artistry of combat that is 52 Blocks.

"A man chosen to wield life and death on the battlefield must be an artist, if he isn't, he is simply a murderer."

Shaka Zulu

The best strategy in this new age of combat is to plan not to over plan. I have noticed in studying combat that everything that is taught or written becomes predictable. The reason behind the predictability is the rigid minds that think of combat as an exact math equation and not an artistic freestyle rap. In real combat there is only one real rule, win at all costs'! I see the ways of today's combat community is to put everyone in a neat little box. There is always a neat spot for you to fit in. This also means you are expected to be a part of the predictability puzzle. But we as true warriors shouldn't fit in any puzzle. In combat you should never be a part of the controlled, organized and regulated rule makers who spend their time making sure you are not self-expressive, so they can have you figured out and feel safe fighting you. I see this in all systems and fighting communities, that believe that their way of combat is the only way. But even in these groups, there is always someone that comes along and scrambles the establishment. Such warriors as Bruce Lee, Muhammad Ali, Roy Jones Jr., Mike Tyson, Cung Lee, Anderson Silva, Jon "Bones" Jones, and Dennis Newsome. These men were and are puzzle scramblers. True warriors are never pieces of the puzzle but are puzzle scramblers. So, let us take off the jacket of predictability. Whether you are a street warrior or a professional fighter, never let others stop you from being a free-flowing, expressive warrior.

Effortless Effort

_____A 52 man must go into combat with the mindset of becoming the fight. One must not be in the moment, but actually be the fight itself. This is done when we learn to improvise during the fight like a Jazz musician playing his set. If a so-called mistake is made that mistake becomes the new technique at that instant. We must remember that 100% of a mistake is better than 50% of the technique, because when you give your all something good will always manifest. But 50% will always be a half-ass effort. The best effort is effortless effort, this is manifested when we become the very thing we are doing. This is called becoming the experience when you are the thing. There is no effort just an honest expression of the is you have become.

"I have known and trained with Diallo Frazier for the past 8 years. His style of 52 Blocks is second to none. When I first saw his skills, I knew right away he was no joke. I have Black Belts in multiple disciplines. Seeing 52 by Diallo made me a believer in this system. His style of 52 Blocks is a complete combative system that was created in slavery, mastered in prison, and perfected on the streets. Diallo's interpretation of 52 Blocks is a well thought out system of defensive attacks, disciplined mindset, and spiritual unity. 52 is a true Black American, bonafide Martial Art System that is complete from philosophy to its history. It is an intelligent and practical style that blends the best of combat systems. It is vicious, smart, to the point, and very effective when practiced in the true spirit of 52. I see Diallo Frazier as a great student and teacher of this amazing style."

Shihan Mark Para, Founder and Chief Instructor of House of Champions in Van Nuys, Ca U.S.A

34 years studying and training in Martial Arts 7th Degree Black Belt, and also holds the title of "BMF."

Warrior's Salute

I would like to give thanks to the Most High first and a warrior salute to all those who have inspired me and have helped the growth of 52 Blocks.

Shihan Mark Para for giving me the idea to write this book and giving me a forum to showcase 52 Blocks at the House of Champions in Van Nuys, Ca.

Larenz Tate for being a disciple of the physical as well as the philosophical 52 Blocks.

Juan Hooks for your dedication to the Art of 52

Chris "Ludacris" Bridges for helping take 52 to another level

Reggie "Rock" Bythewood for having the Strength to bring the Nubian

Amerikan combat system to the world by featuring it in the T.V movie, "Gun Hill."

Senior Master Sergeant (USAF) David Frazier for challenging me to be great.

Seddrick Murray for your Hood Philosophy.

Derrick Morgan for your Hood Spirituality.

Juma Mshabazi for your Virginia Scufflin' Wisdom.

Bruce Dotson for your Friendship.

Big Ant for your 52 and Street Knowledge

Dennis Newsome for your pioneering Spirit and bringing 52 to the world in "Lethal Weapon 1"

Finally, my children, Nkenge and Na'ila for the motivation to make them proud of their father.

And to all those 52 Blocks practitioners past, present, and future know that together we are all bricklaying the foundations for a strong 52 Blocks Nation. Let us build in unity so our building will never crumble.

Peace and Awareness to the "Have Not Nation"

Peace to the most famous Ancestors of Virginia Scuffling turned prizefighters in England.

Tom Malineaux- born a slave in Virginia 1784-1818

Bill Richmond- born a slave in Cuckold Town, Staten Island, New York 1763- 1829

Both of these men found their freedom through Virginia Scufflin', we can still find our freedom through the practicing of the evolved art 52 Hand Blocks.

Triple 7 Salute to:

The Mother of my children, Ericka Sanders

Author Queen Brown

Max Yergan Frazier

Faith Ross

Jacov Bresler

Mel Franklin

Rick Sands

B.J Ingram

Eddie Mendez

Cesar Meji

Derion "D.C" Chapman

Hugo Aranda

Andre Bridges

Assata Shakur

Afeni Shakur

Mumia Abu-Jamal

Dr. Mutulu Shakur

Professor Jamal Joseph

Tupac Shakur

Bunchy Carter

Ken Levine

Lee Caplin

The struggle continues!

"I walk 52 Blocks, so I don't have to carry a Glock 9 or 11. Our strength comes from the number 7."

Diallo Frazier, "Hood Hieroglyphics."

Made in the USA
Columbia, SC
27 September 2020